# GIRLS ROCK!

# Cooking Catastrophe

## Holly Smith Dinbergs

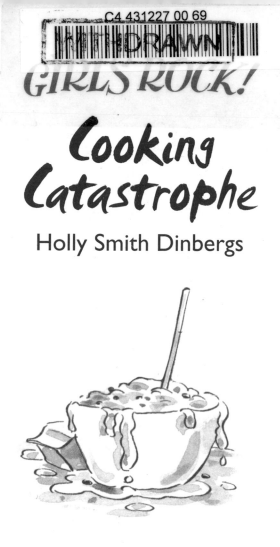

illustrated by

## Chantal Stewart

RISING STARS

First Published in Great Britain by
RISING STARS UK LTD 2006
22 Grafton Street, London, W1S 4EX

For more information visit our website at:
www.risingstars-uk.com

British Library Cataloguing in Publication Data
A CIP record for this book is available from the British Library.

ISBN: 978-1-84680-064-1

First published in 2006 by
MACMILLAN EDUCATION AUSTRALIA PTY LTD
627 Chapel Street, South Yarra 3141

Visit our website at www.macmillan.com.au or go directly to
www.macmillanlibrary.com.au

Associated companies and representatives throughout the world.

Copyright © Holly Smith Dinbergs, Felice Arena and Phil Kettle 2006

Series created by Felice Arena and Phil Kettle
Project management by Limelight Press Pty Ltd
Cover and text design by Lore Foye
Illustrations by Chantal Stewart
Printed in China

UK Editorial by Westcote Computing Editorial Services

# GIRLS ROCK!
# Contents

*Jess*      *Sophie*

# CHAPTER 1

# Who Needs a Recipe?

Jess is at Sophie's house for the afternoon and the girls are chatting. They want to do something but they're not sure what.

**Jess** "I'm hungry. Has your Mum baked any bickies lately?"

**Sophie** "Yes, yesterday. But they've already gone. The 'bottomless pit' ate them, of course."

**Jess** (puzzled) "The bottomless pit?"

**Sophie** "My brother. He eats everything in sight. I have to hide biscuits, or I don't get any."

**Jess** "Got any hidden around here?"

Jess looks under the cushion on the chair and pulls open a drawer in the small side table.

**Sophie** "Nope. But we could make some."

**Jess** "Yes? You're allowed? Your Mum's not home."

**Sophie** "It's OK. Mum showed me how, as long as we remember two things— clean up the mess and don't burn the house down."

**Jess** "Cool, I love baking."

**Sophie** "You mean you love eating!"

**Jess** "Yes, that too!"

**Sophie** "Let's see what we've got."

Sophie heads into the kitchen. She opens the cupboard and pulls out anything that might be good in the biscuits.

**Jess** "I'll get a couple of eggs from the fridge."

Jess opens the fridge door and grabs an egg in each hand.

**Jess**  "Hey Sophie, watch this!"

Jess juggles the eggs, tossing them from one hand to the other.

**Sophie**  "I didn't know you could juggle."

**Jess**  "Neither did I! I'm pretty good, don't you think?"

*Splat*! An egg falls on the floor.

**Jess** (blushing) "Oops. I'll clean it up."

She takes a paper towel and pushes the egg around the floor.

**Jess** "Yuk. This is really slimy. Which recipe are we using, Sophie?"

**Sophie** "We don't need one. You just mix everything, then cook it. It's easy."

# CHAPTER 2

# Ladies and Gentlemen ...

Sophie goes over to the oven while Jess washes her hands.

**Sophie** "Mum always preheats the oven when she's baking. Can you hold the measuring jug while I get the mixing bowl?"

**Jess** "I'll put the flour in first. We'll need at least two cups."

Jess fills the measuring jug to the brim and empties it into the bowl.

**Sophie** "That doesn't look enough. Add a bit more. We want loads of bickies."

**Jess**  "Yes, good idea!"

Jess pours more flour straight from the bag into the bowl. Sophie tips in some sugar and then picks up the salt.

**Sophie**  "We need just a bit of salt."
**Jess**  "I feel like one of those celebrity chefs on a TV cooking show."

Jess grabs a metal whisk and uses it like a microphone.

**Jess** *"Ladies and Gentlemen, today we are lucky to have master chefs Sophie and Jess, who are going to show us how to make the best bickies in the world."*

Jess sticks the whisk in front of Sophie's face, as she pretends to interview her.

**Jess** "*Chef Sophie, you seem to be cooking up a treat. What's the secret of good biscuits?*"

**Sophie** "*Oh, I can't say. That would be breaking the secret cook's code.*"

**Jess** "*How about just a hint, oh great chef Sophie—what's your secret ingredient?*"

**Sophie** "*Er ... lots of flour. Yes, that's it. Loads of flour to make lots of bickies.*"

Jess pours in the last bit of flour.

**Jess** "It's ready to mix now. We can
use the electric mixer for that."
**Sophie** "Yes, OK."

Sophie plugs in her Mum's hand-
mixer. She lowers the mixer into the
bowl and turns it on to "High". Clouds
of flour explode from the bowl!

# CHAPTER 3

# Let It Snow!

The girls cough and laugh, all
at once, as the flour dust covers
everything. Jess pretends to choke.

**Jess** "Wow! It's snowing."
**Sophie** "More like a blizzard!"
**Jess** "It reminds me of when we
went snowboarding last winter—
remember? It was snowing so hard,
we couldn't see anything."

**Sophie** "I remember you almost crashed into that boy!"

**Jess** "Yes, what a nightmare!"

The girls giggle as they brush the flour off themselves.

**Jess** "Oh look, Puffles is making paw prints in the flour."

**Sophie** "Out of the way Puffles, or you might end up in the biscuits!"

**Jess** "Hey, I know why the flour exploded. We forgot to add the wet stuff—the stuff that makes it creamy."

**Sophie** "Oh yes!"

The girls add the egg, butter, milk, peanut butter and chocolate chips to the bowl.

**Jess** "Hey Sophie, remember that
time we made chocolate crispies?"

**Sophie** "Yes, and we put coffee in
the bowl instead of chocolate!"

**Jess** "They were more like coffee
cough drops than chocolate
crispies!"

The girls laugh again.

**Jess** "I know a better way to mix up
the ingredients."

Jess rubs her hands together as Sophie watches in disbelief.

**Sophie** "Are you serious?"

**Jess** "Yes, how do you think they mixed things before mixers were invented?"

Smiling, Jess shoves both her hands into the bowl, squelching the mixture between her fingers.

**Jess** "Plus, this way, you get to taste all the bickie mixture you want."

Jess continues to mix as both girls keep tasting the mixture.

**Sophie** "I think it's mixed enough. If you keep tasting like that we won't have enough left for any bickies! Come on. I'll get out the baking tray."

Jess picks up the heavy bowl. She takes a step, but slips on a bit of the slimy egg left on the floor. *Crash!* She falls backwards and drops the bowl.

**Sophie** "Jess, are you OK?"

**Jess** "Yes, just covered in cake gunk."

**Sophie** "Hey, wait a minute, I can smell smoke."

# CHAPTER 4

# Where There's Smoke

Jess gets up from the floor. The girls sniff the air.

**Jess** "Yes. I smell smoke, too. Where's it coming from?"

Sophie looks around, like a detective searching for a clue.

**Sophie** "It's coming from the oven."

**Jess** "But we haven't put anything in there. Should we call the fire brigade?"

**Sophie** "Don't panic yet!"

**Jess** "I'm not panicking, Sophie. I just smell smoke. Understand? Smoke? Fire? Danger?"

Sophie looks through the glass door of the oven.

**Sophie** "I don't see any fire."

**Jess** "Then why is it smoking?"

**Sophie** "I don't know. I'll open the door."

**Jess** "Are you sure? Wait a minute. I'll turn on the oven light so you can see a bit better."

Jess pushes the button and the oven light comes on.

**Sophie**  "Phew. No fire."

She pulls open the door and smoke pours out.

**Jess**  "Smells like … cheese … tomatoes … something Italian. Spaghetti? Burnt spaghetti?"

**Sophie**  "No. Pizza. It's pizza. My brother was hungry last night, of course, so he made pizza."

Using oven gloves, Sophie removes the tray from the oven.

**Sophie** "This is his dirty dish. He *never* cleans up. See that black lump? That's burned cheese."

**Jess** "It really stinks. My Mum would explode if I left that in there."

**Sophie** "I think mine will too when she sees this."

**Jess** "Wow! Talk about baked on. That stuff will never come off."

**Sophie** "My brother's really in for it. Wait till Mum hears about this. She'll make him clean it up and he won't be impressed."

**Jess** "Yes, boys always make a mess but they never clean it up!"

**Sophie** "Better get this lump of charcoal into the sink."

Jess turns on the tap. When the cold water hits the dish, there's a loud hiss. Water sprays all over the girls. A cloud of steam rises above the sink.

**Jess** "First we had a blizzard, then smoke and now this. It's like three seasons in one day, right here in your kitchen."

# CHAPTER 5

# **Bickie Blunder**

Sophie and Jess sit staring at the timer on the kitchen table, waiting for their biscuits to bake. They have cleaned up their mess and opened the window to get rid of the burnt smell.

**Sophie** "I'm glad we could rescue enough mixture to at least make *some* bickies. They smell great!"

**Jess** "Yes, I'm so hungry."

27

**Sophie** "The timer's going to ring any second."

Jess's foot taps nervously on the floor. Puffles jumps onto a kitchen chair and watches them. *Ding! Ding! Ding!*

**Jess** "Finally!"

With the oven gloves back on, Sophie takes out the baking tray and puts it on a chopping board.

**Jess** "What happened? These bickies look weird."

**Sophie** "What do you mean 'bickies'?" Looks like one big bickie to me."

**Jess** "They've all melted together. And it's really black around the edges."

**Sophie** "Yes, but that doesn't matter. It's how it tastes."

Using a fork, Sophie tries to break up the biscuit, but she can't.

**Sophie** "It's really hard. Like cement."
**Jess** "Here, let me try."

Jess takes the fork and scoops, then stabs at it. Nothing works.

**Sophie** "We could try a hammer. That might break it up."
**Jess** "Mmm … maybe. I think we could build a house with this thing, it's so heavy."

Looking disappointed, the girls stare at the baking tray.

**Sophie** "After all that, we've ended up with nothing at all. Making bickies isn't as easy as it looks."

**Jess** (sighing) "Maybe we should have followed a recipe."

**Sophie** (starting to smile) "We did. A recipe for disaster!"

The girls break into giggles.

**Jess** "Let's leave this brick bickie for your brother. He'd eat anything, especially after it takes him all day to clean up his mess."

**Sophie** "Good idea! Come on. Maybe we can't make the best bickies in the world, but we can buy some!"

# GIRLS ROCK!
## Cooking Lingo

*Jess*

*Sophie*

**à la** A French phrase that means "in the style of", so "bickies à la Sophie" means bickies the way Sophie makes them.

**baking tray** A flat metal tray you use to cook things on in the oven.

**fire extinguisher** What every kitchen needs—just in case something catches fire.

**mix** The food—not the music! When you beat or stir two or more ingredients until they are completely combined.

**whisk** The cooking utensil that you use to make something fluffy, like when you turn gooey egg whites into stiff white peaks for meringue.

# GIRLS ROCK!

# Cooking Must-dos

☆ Make sure your Mum or Dad says it's OK for you to cook if they are not home.

☆ Get everything you will need (ingredients and utensils) before you start. It's much easier!

☆ Check to see that the oven is empty before you turn it on, to avoid any smoky surprises later!

☆ Understand fire safety. If there's a fire in your kitchen, get out and call for help—either your parents or the fire brigade.

☆ Wear oven gloves when you handle anything hot.

☆ Wash your hands before you cook anything (would you want to eat something cooked by someone with dirty hands?).

☆ Make sure you turn off the oven or hob when you have finished cooking.

☆ When baking biscuits or a cake, mix the wet ingredients (like butter and eggs) together first, then slowly add the dry ingredients (like flour and sugar) until the mixture is nice and creamy with no lumps.

☆ If you burn yourself, run very cold water over the burned spot for a couple of minutes. If it's a bad burn, see a doctor.

# GIRLS ROCK!
## Cooking Instant Info

Biscuits were created by accident. The first biscuits were meant just as an oven temperature test. Early bakers used very small amounts of cake batter to test their oven temperatures before baking the final cake.

The world's biggest bag of biscuits was made in Canada in 2001. It took over 11 hours to fill the bag with 100,152 chocolate chip bickies—yum!

The first biscuits are thought to be from the 600s (we live in the 2000s so that was a long time ago) and came from the country that is now known as Iran.

The largest cake on record, baked in Alabama in the United States in 1989, weighed almost 58,000 kilograms.

Biscuits are eaten all over the world but are named differently. "Biscuits" is the name used in Britain and Australia. They are called "cookies" in the United States and "galletas" in Spain. In Italy there are several names, including "biscotti".

The largest pizza in the world was made in South Africa in 1990. The pizza measured over 37 metres in diameter. The crust contained over 4,500 kilograms of flour.

# GIRLS ROCK!
## Think Tank

**1**  What's the best kind of bickie?

**2**  Where do you bake things?

**3**  Name two ways to mix up a cake mix.

**4**  What would you call biscuits if you lived in Canada?

**5**  How big was the world's biggest pizza?

**6**  What do you do if there's a fire in the kitchen?

**7**  How do you make egg whites stiff for meringue desserts?

**8**  How many bickies were in the world's biggest bag of biscuits?

# Answers

1  The best kind of bickie is the one you like the best!

2  You bake things in an oven.

3  You can use a mixer or your hands to mix up a cake mix.

4  If you lived in Canada, you would call biscuits "cookies".

5  The world's biggest pizza measured more than 37 metres across.

6  If there's a fire in the kitchen, get out of the house and call for help—either your parents or the fire brigade!

7  If your dessert recipe calls for meringue, use a whisk to beat the egg whites and make them stiff.

8  The world's biggest bag of biscuits held 100,152 bickies!

# How did you score?

- If you got all 8 answers correct, you should go to catering college and become a world-famous chef.

- If you got 6 answers correct, you should take a cookery class and work for one of the greatest chefs in the world.

- If you got fewer than 4 answers correct, you should buy a cookbook and eat out a lot!

Hey Girls!

I love to read and hope you do, too. The first book I really loved was a book called "Mary Poppins." It was full of magic (way before Harry Potter) and it got me hooked on reading. I went to the library every Saturday and left with a pile of books so heavy I could hardly carry them!

Here are some ideas about how you can make "Cooking Catastrophe" even more fun. At school, you and your friends can be actors and put on this story as a play. To bring the story to life, bring in some props from home such as a mixing bowl, a whisk and a baking tray, and wear aprons.

Who will be Sophie? Who will be Jess? Who will be the narrator? (That's the person who reads the parts between Jess or Sophie saying something.) Once you've decided on these details, you're ready to act out the story in front of the class. I bet everyone will clap when you are finished. Hey, a talent scout from a television channel might just be watching!

See if somebody at home will read this story out loud with you. Reading at home is important and a lot of fun as well.

You know what my Dad used to tell me? "Readers are leaders!"

And, remember, Girls Rock!

## GIRLS ROCK!
## When We Were Kids

*Holly*  *Jacqueline*

Holly talked to Jacqueline, another *Girls Rock!* author.

**Jacqueline** "Did you like to cook when you were a kid?"

**Holly** "Yes, I had a toy oven. It cooked things with the heat from a light bulb."

**Jacqueline** "A light bulb?"

**Holly** "Yes. It got really hot. I made little white cakes."

**Jacqueline** "What happened if the light bulb went out?"

**Holly** "It got dark ... so the cakes turned to chocolate!"

# GIRLS ROCK!

# What a Laugh!

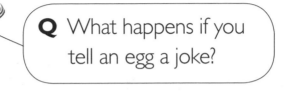

**Q** What happens if you tell an egg a joke?

**A** It cracks up!

# GiRLS ROCK!

The Sleepover

Pool Pals

Bowling Buddies

Girl Pirates

Netball Showdown

School Play Stars

Diary Disaster

Horsing Around

Newspaper Scoop

Snowball Attack

Dog on the Loose

Escalator Escapade

Cooking Catastrophe

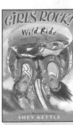
Talent Quest

Wild Ride

Camping Chaos

Mummy Mania

Skater Chicks

**GiRLS ROCK!** books are available from most booksellers. For mail order information please call Rising Stars on 0870 40 20 40 8 or visit www.risingstars-uk.com